Dad is moving on; Masculinity and Mental Health

TABLE OF CONTENT

INTRODUCTION

We hear about it all the time the rate of divorce is rising, children are being separated and are collateral damage, the men go through a lot holding the balance with little to no appreciation, especially when dealing with physiological breakdown

This read is a full step by step guide to men struggling with divorce, managing your mental health as a man, overcoming the stereotype and living up to a better version of yourself.

Dad is moving on; Masculinity and Mental Health

Chapter 1

About Psychological well-being

Our way of life doesn't necessarily in all cases pass on space for men to communicate internal battle.

For men specifically, who've been told for their entire lives to "man up" and be solid, getting to psychological wellness assets can appear to conflict with social assumptions.

However, throughout recent years, there's been developing activism and interest around the subject of male psychological well-being, halfway on account of those in the media spotlight who've been vocal about their own encounters. Society lets men know that it's essentially not satisfactory have an excessive number of sentiments. It's so critical to shout out and battle shame. This is the thing I maintain that others should be aware, including what it's prefer to have a psychological wellness determination, how to request help, and what they figure the eventual fate of men's emotional well-being will resemble

1. There are a lot of reasons men don't search out help, regardless of whether they need i it frequently feels like you are the main individual who apparently can't deal with it. You lay there restlessly around evening time alone, asking why you can't be as in charge as you ought to be and frantically doing whatever it takes not to let any other individual perceive how you are truly doing."

2. Some of the time, regardless of whether you realize you want assistance, it very well may be hard to know where to begin. "I've encountered numerous men who would rather not request help since they're anxious about looking frail or inept," says Timothy Wenger, a men's emotional well-being proficient and blogger at The Man Impact. This is the kind of thing I'm looking out to change. I believe men should realize that their conflicts under the surface are similarly all around as substantial as some other battle, and these don't make them to a lesser extent a man. What I'm finding, however, is numerous men don't have any idea how to request help."

3. And keeping in mind that observing an advisor is hard and may take a few experimentations, it's eventually worth the effort. "Nonetheless, it was the exact inverse! I thought, 'What is an advisor going to let me know that I don't as of now have the foggiest idea?' After impressive inciting from two dear companions, I chose to plan my first arrangement. Sadly, that specific advisor was

certifiably not a solid match - rashly affirming to me that I knew everything. However, I was all the while battling with habit. Fortunately, my guide provoked me to visit a particular specialist. My underlying visit to that advisor transformed me and eventually assisted me with figuring out things for myself."

4. Also, seeking he can take many structures.

"It's great to remember that 'requesting help' isn't generally a relentless, troublesome undertaking," says Matt Mahalo, a creator and speaker who has managed his own emotional wellness battles. Again, something as Blunt as a couple of hours fishing recuperation stories and tips on YouTube can be to the point of kicking you off headed for recuperation. In some cases, it goes on a basic outing to the library. For instance, my first huge advance forward occurred while perusing 'The Specialty of Joy.'"

5. Individuals frequently feel an enormous liberating sensation after at long last telling others what they're going through. This incorporates artist Zayn Malik, who as of late opened up to the world about his encounters with nervousness and a dietary issue. At any point which you feel like you're keeping something from somebody. You need to talk about it and clear up the air," he let us know Week after week in a meeting.

6. Emotional well-being issues are much more normal. Emotional well-being issues are much more normal than you might think, however by making some noise, a few men are attempting to bring issues to light.

I've had about six discouragement spells that I've gone through. Furthermore, the one of every 2014, I would have rather not been alive," Michael Phelps told TODAY. Taking into account that 1 out of 5 U.S. grown-ups experience an emotional well-being condition at whatever year, it's significant that these issues get standardized - and that is by and large why Phelps made it a highlight share his involvement in others. "You know, as far as I might be concerned, I essentially conveyed pretty much every pessimistic feeling you might conceivably convey along for 15-20 years and I never discussed it. Furthermore, I don't have the foggiest idea why that one day I chose to simply open up. Yet, since that day, it's simply been such a ton more straightforward to live thus a lot simpler to appreciate life and it's something I'm extremely grateful for," Phelps said.

7. Emotional well-being issues can be difficult to truly comprehend on the off chance that you haven't encountered them yourself. In his tune "In My Blood," pop star Shawn Mendes stands up to his own encounters with nervousness, singing, "Help me, it resembles the dividers are collapsing. Here and there I want to surrender. "Conversing with Beats 1 about the tune, he said, "It was somewhat something that hit me inside the last year. Before that, growing up, I was a quiet child, very consistent. "He likewise noticed that it tends to be difficult to really get what individuals living with uneasiness are going through until you experience it

yourself. "I knew individuals who had experienced nervousness and tracked down it sort of difficult to comprehend, however at that point when it hits you, you're like, 'Good gracious, what is this? This is insane,'" he said.

8. The way that superstars appear to be increasingly more open to discussing their psychological wellness is additionally uplifting, some of the time in any event, putting an entertaining twist on what it is prefer to live with a dysfunctional behavior. In 2017, Pete Davidson of Saturday Night Live focused on his encounters with ongoing sadness and his new determination of marginal behavioral condition Despondency influences in excess of 16 million individuals in this nation and there's no fix

in essence, yet for anybody managing it, there are medicines that can help. Most importantly, assuming that you believe you're discouraged, see a specialist and converse with them about drug. And furthermore, be sound. Eating right and exercise can have a gigantic effect," Davidson suggested. He went on happily: At long last, assuming you're in the cast of a late-night satire show, it would be ideal if they, you know, accomplish a greater amount of your improv shows.

9. With or without jokes, specialists in this field have a confident viewpoint. As more men (particularly those in the public eye) stand up against their battles and involvement in psychological well-being challenges,

others can see that the battle is genuine and you are in good company.

We can keep on spreading mindfulness and standardize the way that it tends to be hard to oversee pressure and ordinary requests, he brings up. In particular, we really want to keep on receiving out the message of trust, Gonzalez says. There are compelling psychotherapy medicines and meds that can assist with overseeing pressure, uneasiness, discouragement, and other emotional wellness issues. Men's emotional wellness is a significant yet frequently disregarded wellbeing concern. All kinds of people experience emotional wellness troubles. Notwithstanding, there are a few striking contrasts between the issues influencing them and the

elements that impact those issues.

Continue to peruse to study the most well-known issues

and conditions influencing men's psychological well-

being, including expected medicines and ways of helping

other people encountering emotional well-being issues

Chapter 2

The social standard

What psychological wellness issues mean for men in an unexpected way, seeking help is a significant initial phase in recuperating from any psychological well-being condition. Contrasts in condition pervasiveness and self-destruction rates. Ladies are more likely Trusted Source to encounter emotional well-being conditions than men. They are likewise more likely Trusted Source to endeavor self-destruction. Notwithstanding, men are more than 3.5 times bound to kick the bucket from self-destruction than ladies. This might be on the grounds that they will more often than not pick more deadly weapons, like guns.

Different affecting elements

Men's issues can create from various causes and triggers than those that influence ladies.

For instance, men's issues frequently originate from cultural assumptions and conventional orientation jobs, which might lead men to believe that they should:

•   be the providers in the family

•   show customary manly qualities, like strength and control

•   depend on oneself and not look for help from others

•   not talk transparently about their feelings

Clutching these conventional convictions can adversely affect men's psychological wellness and hold them back from getting to help and treatment. Men are definitely less likely Trusted Source than ladies to look for treatment for issues, for example, wretchedness, substance misuse, and unpleasant life occasions. As per Psychological wellness America, this is expected to:

- social standards

- a hesitance to talk

- making light of their side effects

A Public Wellbeing Interview Review reports that only 1 out of 3 men took more time for day-to-day sensations of gloom or tension, while only 1 out of 4 addressed a psychological well-being

Cautioning signs

The signs and side effects Believed Wellspring of a psychological well-being condition will rely upon the kind, yet there are a few side effects that individuals can pay special attention to. These include:

- forcefulness, outrage, and crabbiness

- changes in mind-set or energy levels

- changes in craving or resting propensities

- trouble centering

- feeling anxious or "tense"

- a maximum usage of liquor

- improper utilization of medications

- partaking in unsafe exercises

- feeling miserable, irredeemable, numb, or inwardly
level

- having throbs, torments, or other actual side effects without an unmistakable reason

- over the top or urgent contemplations or ways of behaving

- thinking or acting such that makes concern others or contrarily affects work, social, or everyday life

- contemplating or endeavoring self destruction

In the event that an individual notification these side effects in themselves or then again assuming a friend or family member spots them, it is really smart to look for clinical assistance. Treating emotional wellness issues in the beginning phases can frequently keep the side effects from turning out to be more serious and bring down the gamble of intricacies.

Who is in danger?   A few elements increment the gamble of emotional well-being conditions and self-destruction among men. The accompanying gatherings might be more in danger than others:

• More established, white men: White men matured 85 years and more seasoned are most in danger of self-destruction. More men in this segment kick the bucket by self-destruction consistently than in some other gathering by age, sex, or race

• Men encountering business issues: Working in unfortunate circumstances or having a high responsibility can expand the gamble of emotional wellness issues. Joblessness and retirement likewise increment the risk Trusted Wellspring of despondency and self-destruction.

• Men who have had a conjugal breakdown: Misery is more normal, and more serious, among men who are separated. One study Trusted Source recommends that being single is a huge self-destruction trigger among men.

• Men with lawful or monetary worries: Having legitimate or monetary concerns can set off the improvement of emotional well-being issues and increment the gamble of self-destruction.

• Men who abuse liquor or medications: Men are more likely Trusted Source to participate in unlawful medication use and liquor use, which can set off or worsen psychological wellness conditions.

• Men with a family background of psychological well-being issues: Numerous mental circumstances - including bipolar turmoil, wretchedness, and schizophrenia - run in families Trusted Source, recommending a hereditary part.

- Men managing other life challenges: Other gamble factors Trusted Source for emotional well-being issues and self-destruction incorporate actual sickness or inconvenience, struggle with family or companions, and the disease or demise of a relative.

.

-

Chapter 3

Getting How Men Grieve

Men should be solid. That is everything society has said to us for ages. Indeed, even as society's assumptions have step by step different, numerous men actually attempt to stay apathetic in any event, when they experience a profound, individual misfortune. Understanding how men lament can assist men with understanding their own feelings and assist the people who with cherishing them to offer the help they need in a troublesome time.

Side effects of Grief in Men

Melancholy is a special encounter. It is interesting to every person. Each misfortune that singular experiences is capable in an unexpected way. Whenever we consider lamenting, the vast majority of us believe bitterness and crying to be regular. Yet, there are numerous side effects of anguish. For men used to concealing tears, different side effects can be more normal. These include:

•	Withdrawal - Many men will pull out from loved ones, both truly and inwardly, when they are lamenting.

• Crabbiness - Men who have encountered a misfortune might be all the more effectively aggravated by little disturbances.

• Outrage - Men who are in grieving can encounter outrage at those they see as liable for their cherished one's passing, at themselves, or even at nothing specifically. They can blow up and detonate over little issues that normally wouldn't annoy them.

• Steady Thoughts of Death - This incorporates pondering the deficiency of their cherished one, the last snapshots of their passing or demise overall.

• Substance Abuse - Men who are grieving may endeavor to veil their aggravation with liquor or medications. I see various articulations of pain paying little heed to orientation," Crossroads Hospice and Palliative Care Bereavement Coordinator David Stephenson shares. I converse with men in tears and ladies who pull out into hecticness. Every individual is special.

There is no correct method for lamenting. Men might encounter some or none of the side effects of melancholy above. Men might encounter a time of extreme sorrow or more gentle side effects of anguish. The sort of despondency experienced can fluctuate generally, no matter what their relationship with their cherished one.

Men are bound to lament in disengagement. Assuming that a male cherished one is grieving a misfortune, you can help by telling them you are there to tune in and support them when they are prepared to talk. Allow it to occur on their conditions.

One more method for aiding is to chip away at an undertaking with them that is inconsequential to their misfortune or join your male adored one on a long vehicle trip or a day of fishing. He might wind up discussing his misfortune. He may not. Yet, basically he will have your consistent friendship and backing.

Men frequently will seek after exercises to occupy them from pondering their anguish. This is useful for certain men, yet for other people, trying not to ponder the misfortune can prompt a more extended and more convoluted distress process.

One method for aiding is recommend an undertaking your adored one can deal with that praises the person who has died. This could be establishing a tree, taking an interest in an infection mindfulness walk, or in any event, constructing an aviary committed to their cherished one's memory. Accomplishing something active with a useful objective can be staggeringly mending for men who observe fixing things fulfilling.

I have seen a great deal of progress in the manner people lament," adds David. Years prior, individuals would go to the burial ground to lament. Presently, it's more liquid. Families will set up recognitions with photographs or other keepsakes in their home or their vehicle. It is more significant to them, and they process their sorrow regularly as opposed to compartmentalizing it.

We as a whole have a decision. We can zero in on the passing or generally that the individual brought to the world while they were alive.

Relationship and Psychological well-being

The new review expresses that relationship changes in men increment the gamble of psychological maladjustments like discouragement, uneasiness, and self-destruction.

Most men encountered the beginning or deteriorating of psychological instability side effects during a bothered relationship or following the breakdown of a relationship,

Hazard of Psychological sickness

The review at UBC's Men's Wellbeing Exploration Program cross examined 47 men in regards to their breakdown encounters with a close accomplice relationship.

It was noticed that the gamble of male self-destruction nearly quadruples after conjugal partition. One reason for expanded risk among men is expected to the minimize issues declared by men, which prompts significantly further harms to the relationship.

Break the Generalizations

Generalized manliness assumes a part in how men respond to a wrecked relationship. For instance, men's vulnerability for how to expressive and issue settle in the relationship setting brought about numerous men detaching instead of connecting for help.

It was observed that troubled men utilized substances and liquor? to adapt to their separation sentiments like annoyance, trouble, lament, culpability, and disgrace. Besides, the vulnerability of life, loss of social associations, general wellbeing limitations, and monetary difficulties confuse the trouble much more.

Cultivate Positive Strength

Notwithstanding, optimistically speaking, the concentrate additionally uncovered the commitment of men in an assortment of assets after the relationship breakdown for additional tending to the psychological wellness needs.

Help-chasing endeavors among these men were wide-going and included individual or singular endeavors like activity, perusing and taking care of oneself while different men tapped existing organizations or stretched out their endeavors to associate with help gatherings, or went to treatment," says Gabriela Montaner, the task lead and co-writer on the article.

The concentrate in this way expresses those men should dedicate significant work to continue on from the separation instead of having a tendency to sit tight until emergency for looking for help.

The discoveries in this way lay forward significant settings to develop better connections among men.

Adapting To Division and Separation

Going through a detachment or separation can be undeniably challenging, no great explanation for it. It can flip around your reality and make it difficult to overcome the work day and remain useful. Be that as it may, there are things you can do to overcome this troublesome change.

Perceive that having various feelings' alright. It's generally expected to feel miserable, furious, depleted, disappointed and confounded and these sentiments can be extraordinary. You additionally may have a restless outlook on what's to come. Acknowledge that responses like these will decrease after some time. Regardless of whether the marriage was unfortunate, wandering into the obscure is startling.

Offer yourself a reprieve. Allow yourself to feel and to work at a not exactly ideal level for a while. You will be unable to be very as useful at work or care for others in precisely the manner you're familiar with for a brief

period. Nobody is superman or superwoman; take more

time to mend, refocus and recharge

The amass in this manner communicates that men ought to devote critical work to forge ahead from the division as opposed to tending to hold on until crisis for searching for help.

The discover expected to feel hopeless, irate, drained, disheartened and bewildered and these sentiments men and their medical services experts to perceive when they could require psychological well-being support.

Here is the lowdown on everything connected with men's emotional well-being, from recognizing side effects to tracking down the right sort of treatment.

- changes in hunger and energy

- new a throbbing painfulness

- stomach related issues

- inconvenience dozing

- dozing more than expected

Frequently, loved ones might be the initial ones to see the side effects, as it tends to be challenging to remember them while you're encountering them.

 Men are more averse to have gotten emotional well-being treatment than ladies in the previous year.

This doesn't mean men don't need or profit from treatment.

Rather, men can find it more troublesome being open about their emotional well-being and looking for help since it's probably going to conflict with the sorts of messages they got growing up

She proceeds to take note of that many societies have solid social generalizations around how men ought to act, particularly around dealing with their feelings and showing up "solid."

Furthermore, men who don't (or feel that they can't) talk straightforwardly about their sentiments could make some harder memories perceiving the side effects of psychological wellness conditions in themselves

•

Normal emotional well-being conditions in men

The absolute most pervasive psychological wellness conditions among men are:

Gloom

Discouragement is portrayed by a steady low state of mind that impedes ordinary working. Around the world, it is one of the most widely recognized emotional wellness conditions.

Sorrow is two times as common Trusted Source in ladies
as men. Nonetheless, men are definitely less likely
Trusted Source than ladies to look for treatment

Uneasiness problems

Uneasiness problems are described by extraordinary and
wild sensations of dread and stress.

The most widely recognized type, summed up uneasiness
jumble (Stray), frequently co-happens with misery.
Despite the fact that ladies are two times as prone to
encounter Stray, men are more averse to look for
treatment for it.

Different kinds of uneasiness problems, for example,
social tension issue and fanatical enthusiastic issue
(OCD), are similarly normal among people.

Social uneasiness problem causes extraordinary
nervousness and dread in friendly circumstances, while
OCD causes the consistent redundancy of explicit
considerations (fixations) or a habitual need to perform
explicit schedules over and over (impulses).

Schizophrenia

Schizophrenia is a serious emotional well-being condition wherein individuals don't decipher reality all things considered. They experience mind flights, dreams, and different types of cluttered thinking.

Schizophrenia can altogether affect personal satisfaction and connections. Of the people who get a schizophrenia analysis by the age of 30 years, 90% are men.

PTSD

PTSD is a condition described by side effects of remembering a horrible encounter, aversion, and hyperarousal.

Research shows that around 60% of men experience no less than one horrible accident in the course of their life, while half of ladies do. Kinds of injury contrast, with men being bound to encounter:

- mishaps

- attacks

- battle

- cataclysmic events

- seeing a demise or injury

Ladies are bound to encounter rape or kid sexual maltreatment.

In spite of the fact that men have a higher gamble of horrendous accidents, ladies are bound to foster PTSD.

Substance misuse

Across most age gatherings, men have higher rates Trusted Wellspring of use or reliance on unlawful medications and liquor than ladies. They are likewise bound to require a crisis office visit and bite the dust from glut.

As per the Public Foundation on Liquor Misuse and Alcoholism Trusted Source, 68,000 men kick the bucket yearly from liquor related causes, contrasted and 27,000 ladies.

Treatment

Albeit numerous men are hesitant to look for and continue Trusted Source treatment for emotional wellness issues, it is a crucial stage in recuperation. With viable treatment, individuals can figure out how to deal with their side effects and start to feel significantly improved.

Some treatment choices include:

Psychotherapy

Treatment can assist with peopling figure out through problems that have set off emotional wellness conditions. It can likewise assist people with dealing with their side effects, change their pessimistic contemplations and pointless ways of behaving, and acquire new adapting abilities.

There are a wide range of styles of treatment. For it to be compelling, fundamental individuals track down the right advisor and sort of treatment for them.

Prescription

A specialist might endorse drug to treat different emotional well-being conditions or side effects related with those diseases.

For instance, they might endorse:

- antidepressants

- antianxiety prescriptions

- antipsychotic drugs

- tranquilizers

Ordinarily, specialists will suggest that individuals use drugs in mix with psychotherapy.

Way of life changes

Making positive way of life changes can make a critical commitment to mental prosperity.

For instance, it is essential to:

• Eat a decent eating regimen.

• Get sufficient rest.

• Practice as a general rule.

• Oversee pressure through reflection or yoga, or in alternate ways.

• Limit or stay away from the utilization of liquor and medications.

Peer support

Going to a care group or gathering advising can be extremely useful for those with an emotional well-being condition.

Avoidance

There is no certain method for forestalling psychological well-being conditions. Be that as it may, the accompanying advances might diminish the gamble of creating one:

• Speak with loved ones, particularly during distressing periods.

• Look for treatment expeditiously assuming any side effects of poor emotional well-being create.

• Go on with support treatment to forestall backslides of misery or other emotional well-being conditions.

• Figure out how to oversee pressure through contemplation, care, imaginative outlets, or different strategies.

• Practice positive way of life decisions, like eating great, resting enough, and working out.

• See an advisor for issues, for example, low confidence or youth injury, which could set off emotional well-being issues further down the road.

• In the event that somebody is in danger of self destruction, don't let them be. Call 911 and stand by with them until help shows up.

Having the help of friends and family can altogether affect an individual's recuperation. Some research Trusted Source even proposes that certain individuals who have self-destructive contemplations however don't follow up on them decide not to do so due to the help of their loved ones.

•   Hoedspruit, which is an association that gives methodologies to oversee or forestall misery in men

•   the November Establishment, which is a foundation that spotlights on issues that influence men's physical and psychological well-being.

Manage yourself really and in fact. Truly deal with yourself and to your body. Get some vacation to work out, eat well and loosen up. Keep to your commonplace timetables whatever amount as could be anticipated. Endeavor to make an effort not to seek after critical decisions or changes in life plans. Do whatever it takes not to use alcohol, drugs or cigarettes as a strategy for adjusting; they simply lead to more issues.

Avoid battles for control and conflicts with your buddy or past mate. Yet again accepting a discussion begins to change into a fight, calmly suggest that you both make a pass at talking sometime in the future and either leave or hang up the phone.

Invest in some opportunity to explore your tendencies. Reconnect with things you value doing isolated from your soul mate. Have you for the most part expected to take up painting or play in an intramural softball team? Seek after a class, center significantly around your recreation exercises, volunteer, and invest in some opportunity to see the value throughout everyday life and make new associates.

Think strongly. Simple to discuss, not so natural to do, right? Things may not be something basically the same, but finding new activities and associates, and pushing ahead with reasonable suppositions will gain this headway more direct. Be versatile. If you have children, family customs will regardless be critical yet some of them could ought to be changed. Help with making new family works out.

Life will completely recuperate, yet "standard" may be not equivalent to what you had at first trusted.

Ways of talking with kids ...

Accepting you have children, here's a short overview of tips that can help your little children and young people with adjusting.

Control center and tune in. Guarantee your youngsters understand that your detachment isn't their weakness. Focus on and work with their inclinations, and be accommodating anyway direct in your responses.

Stay aware of constancy and timetables. Endeavor to keep your youngsters' regular and step by step plans as normal and consistent as could be anticipated.

Offer unsurprising discipline. Now that your kids could confer time to the two watchmen freely, attempt to agree somewhat early on rest times, curfews and other conventional decisions, as well as any disciplines.

Tell your young people they can rely upon you. Make and keep reasonable certifications. Additionally, don't exorbitantly confide in them about your feelings about the detachment.

Do whatever it takes not to remember your children for the dispute. Make an effort not to fight with or talking unfavorably about the other parent before your youngsters. Do whatever it takes not to include them as spies or messengers, or make them favor one side.

Mental health conditions don't separate. People, things being what they are, can experience trouble, anxiety, and other enthusiastic prosperity conditions. Regardless, they could seem, by all accounts, to be remarkable in men.

Direction speculations and disgrace can moreover make it harder for the two men and their clinical consideration specialists to see when they could require mental prosperity support.

Here is the lowdown on everything associated with men's enthusiastic prosperity, from recognizing aftereffects to finding the right kind of treatment.

Men's enthusiastic prosperity aftereffects to search for

Individuals can occasionally experience a comparable passionate prosperity condition in different ways in view of a mix of natural and social factors.

Mental prosperity secondary effects in men could include:

- shock and forcefulness

- delicateness

- disappointment

- substance misuse

- bother concentrating

- persevering vibes of stress

- responsibility in high-risk works out

- astonishing approach to acting that concerns others or obstructs everyday presence

- considerations of implosion

Some enthusiastic wellbeing conditions, including pressure and despairing, can in like manner have real incidental effects that people could ignore.

These include:

- changes in wanting and energy

- new a pounding difficulty

- stomach related issues

- burden resting

up "strong."

Also, men who don't (or feel that they can't) talk clearly about their opinions could gain a few harder experiences seeing the results of mental prosperity conditions in themselves.

Tracking down help with your mental health

Accepting that you're examining associating for help yet aren't don't have the foggiest idea where to start, you have several options.

Expecting you at this point reliably see a clinical benefits capable, they can be a respectable early phase. Dependent upon their experience, they'll likely suggest you to someone who invests critical energy in mental wellbeing, like a trained professional or clinician

Make specific choices (or send a couple of messages)

Preceding arranging a course of action, contact guides you're enthused about seeing.

Give them some fundamental establishment on what you should address, as well as anything you're looking for in a subject matter expert. Do you want someone who's available for night or week's end plans? The thing may be said about text support in gatherings? Would it be able to be said that you are enthusiastic about endeavoring teletherapy, or would you be able to like eye to eye gatherings?

Expecting you have medical care, this is a cheerful opportunity to get some data about that, also. Treatment isn't by and large covered, yet a couple of counselors will give documentation you can submit to your security provider for reimbursement.

During the game plan

Your counsel will presumably spend the chief gathering or two getting to know you. This is in like manner an opportunity for you to get to know their technique, so create it a highlight any requests around what you can expect from future gatherings.

It's huge you feel open to visiting with the expert you pick. If you feel as, aren't you "clicking" with your consultant after two or three gatherings, you can consistently examine various decisions. A ton of people need to see several counselors before they notice someone who's a strong match.

Dependent upon your incidental effects, your guide could imply you to an expert to research solution, including antidepressants.

Recall that remedy isn't actually something you'll need to take for the rest of your life. A portion of the time, it just gives a momentary lift to help you with starting dealing with the essential purposes behind your aftereffects. An advisor can moreover help you with investigating any accidental impacts you could insight.

Dad is moving on; Masculinity and Mental Health

Chapter 4

Adapting to emotional wellness side effects

Everybody can profit from taking care of oneself, including men. While working with an emotional well-being proficient can be a major assistance, there are a lot of things you can do to help yourself between meetings.

Tournai features diet, rest, and exercise as elements, however makes sense of that "we additionally need to ensure we're caring for our enthusiastic prosperity."

Furthermore, here and there, that implies being "ready to recognize and remain with sentiments - particularly the awkward ones - rather than driving them away or denying them."

Sitting with awkward sentiments is more difficult than one might expect, and that can make it simple to fall into pointless survival techniques, similar to substance use or disregarding feelings.

While both of these could offer a few transient advantages, they won't offer durable alleviation. Now and again, they could even make long haul issues.

The following time you wind up encountering an awkward inclination or feeling, attempt:

- doing a fast body filter contemplation

- working out the thing you're feeling

- rehearsing a few basic breathing strategies

As you explore various approaches to dealing with your feelings, be delicate with yourself. On the off chance that you don't go after the "awesome" survival strategies on an awful day, for instance, don't whip yourself. There will generally be one more chance to rehearse new techniques.

Opening up to companions

Discussing what you're proceeding with a companion can likewise be a major assistance, yet that might be troublesome assuming your companions are additionally men who could struggle with opening up. However, beginning that discussion could turn out to be valuable for both of you.

Mark Meier, the chief overseer of the Face It Establishment, says men actually should figure out how to get the subtleties of feeling and perceive those pessimistic feelings are ordinary and repeating feelings over the course of life.

He suggests getting down somebody that you can talk straightforwardly with about your own difficulties and free yourself up to filling more top to bottom associations with others. Your specialist can absolutely be that individual; however, you could likewise find it accommodating to open up to a companion.

You can take a stab at beginning the discussion with something like, I've been going through a great deal. Do have the opportunity to look up some other time this week?

Assuming you feel available, you can likewise make yourself accessible to a companion deprived with a basic, I saw you've appeared to be somewhat down of late. Simply believe you should know I'm generally accessible to talk on the off chance that you really want it.

Dad is moving on; Masculinity and Mental Health

The reality

Emotional well-being can be difficult to contemplate. Furthermore, recognizing that you're observing it troublesome or that you could require help is generally difficult - especially for men.

In any case, it's ideal to stand up. Whether you open up to a companion or relative or counsel your PCP, there's assist with trip there, and ways of dealing with your psychological wellness yourself, as well.

Powerful Methods for reconstructing Yourself After a Separation and Continue On

Modifying your life after the misery monetary precariousness of separation is conceivable with the tip's underneath.

Remaking yourself after a divorce can be hard. Whenever a relationship that you have contributed a ton of feeling and time closes, it can feel like the finish of your life. You could feel like there won't ever be any expect joy in your life once more.

A separation can leave you completely discouraged, miserable and monetarily shaky. You might feel like you have been flipped around. It is challenging to change and begin living alone and being single once more, particularly assuming that you had been hitched for quite a while. It very well may be challenging to zero in on yourself, however this is an ideal opportunity to push ahead and rediscover who you truly are - regardless of the age.

You might feel like it is difficult to remake yourself after separate - however it's not!

As per Unmistakable, it takes a normal of two years for you to begin feeling typical subsequent to going through an unpleasant separation. During this period, there are a few things you can do that can speed up your mending interaction.

Lament

Separate is like passing. All that you had with your accomplice is before. You share nothing practically speaking at this point. There is something inside you that needs for the life and request you once had. It is exceptionally normal to grieve the way of life you have lost regardless of whether you are the person who started the separation.

Get some much-needed rest to be separated from everyone else and lament. Try not to go looking for one more accomplice to fill the empty space you have inside you. Besides the fact that such connections fall, however they can leave you completely crushed indeed. Being distant from everyone else will assist you with pondering your past and assist you with settling on better choices later on. You will likewise end up turning out to be happier with being separated from everyone else. This has to be the very first step you take. You ought to be happy with being separated from everyone else it first before you can put your time and feelings in another relationship once more.

As per Studies, it takes a fraction of the time you were submitted in the relationship to grieve completely. You will figure out that as days pass, and as you permit yourself to lament, you will continuously give up.

Record it

Continuously have a diary to record your everyday enthusiastic battles. Recording your battles and upsetting encounters can assist you with sorting out your considerations and assume command over your feelings.

By journaling consistently, you can follow your upgrades effectively and motivate yourself to push ahead. Journaling is a vital part of following. Following will empower you to work on an all aspects of your life and assist you with revamping yourself after a separation.

Speak with loved ones There will generally be one more chance to rehearse new techniques.

Powerful Methods for reconstructing Yourself After a Separation and Continue On

Modifying your life after the misery monetary precariousness of separation is conceivable with the tips underneath.

62

Dad is moving on; Masculinity and Mental Health

CHAPTER 5

Conclusion

Men's emotional wellness issues vary from ladies in numerous ways, yet they are similarly as significant. One concerning viewpoint is that men are more hesitant to look for treatment for issues they face. The gamble of self destruction is additionally a lot higher among men.

Notwithstanding, looking for and proceeding with treatment can emphatically affect the existences of men who experience psychological wellness challenges. Looking for help from wellbeing experts and friends and family can facilitate the side effects, work on personal satisfaction, and lessen the gamble of self-destruction.

Numerous associations offer help to those encountering emotional wellness challenges, and many spotlight exclusively on giving data and help to men.